STORY AND ART BY
**YUKINOBU
TATSU**

DANDADAN

7

CHARACTERS

MOMO AYASE

A high school girl from a family of spirit mediums. Her powers awakened after she was abducted by aliens. Following the battle with Turbo Granny, she helps to search for Okarun's testicles.

OKARUN (KEN TAKAKURA)

A geek for paranormal phenomena who lost his testicles in the fight against Turbo Granny and must now spend his time looking for them. He has developed feelings for Momo.

TURBO GRANNY

Appearing at unexpected times and places, she's a present-day yokai who ran riot throughout the country. Her power remains within Okarun, while her consciousness is stuck in a beckoning-cat figure that she uses to get around.

JIJI (JIN ENJOJI)

Momo's friend since childhood. He recruits Momo and Okarun to investigate and exorcise the spirits in his family's new house. But before they can, his body is possessed by the Evil Eye, a boy who'd been sacrificed under the house and became a yokai.

AIRA SHIRATORI

A popular, attractive girl at Momo's school whose powers awaken when she unknowingly picks up one of Okarun's family jewels. She ends up taking on the aura of the Acrobatic Silky.

TARO

An anatomical-model yokai who is dating anatomical model Hana. At present he has Jiji, currently possessed by the Evil Eye, trapped inside his own body.

MANJIRO

A priest at the Tsuchinoko Shrine near Jiji's home. He is also Seiko's disciple.

SEIKO

Momo's grandmother. She's active as the spirit medium Santa Dodoria. She's powerful enough to enclose their home in a mystical barrier, and she supports Momo and the others from the shadows.

STORY

Momo, a firm believer in spirits, comes to the rescue of a paranormal fanatic named Ken Takakura, aka Okarun, when he's getting bullied. After arguing about the validity of each other's interests, they decide to prove their respective beliefs, so Momo is sent to an abandoned hospital known for UFO sightings and Okarun heads to a supposedly haunted tunnel. Once there, Okarun gets cursed by a yokai called Turbo Granny! At the hospital, Momo ends up abducted by aliens called Serpoians, who are seeking a human female for reproduction. They take her aboard their ship, and Momo finds herself in big trouble. Suddenly, Okarun appears, and thanks to Turbo Granny's curse, he's able to transform. At the same time, Momo awakens to her paranormal abilities, and the two are able to escape the UFO. But Okarun's curse affects those around them, so they decide to have a showdown with Turbo Granny. Seiko sets up a barrier around Kamikoshi City, and Momo and Okarun subsequently beat Turbo Granny through a game of tag. Later, Jiji, Momo's old childhood friend and first crush, shows up troubled with supernatural problems of his own occurring in his family's new home, so Okarun and Momo head there to investigate. However, there are legends of a giant serpent in the area. In fact, the Kito clan has been secretly sacrificing humans to it under Jiji's new home, and they toss the young trio into an underground alternate reality as the latest offering. There the three find the serpent as well as a sacrificed child, now an Evil Eye yokai who goes on to possess Jiji. Suddenly, Seiko appears, sealing Jiji's possessed body inside the anatomical-model yokai Taro with a plan to exorcise it. Will Jiji get his body back, or is it too late to separate them?!

DAN DA DAN 7

SO BASICALLY, LIKE, WHAT?

BUT IF IT'S HOT WATER, HE'S JIJI?

IF HE GETS SPLASHED WITH COLD WATER, HE'S THE EVIL EYE?

50. Let's All Carry Around Hot Water

DON'T KNOW WHAT TO DO!

YAPPA PAA YAPPA PAA!

EACH OF YOU...

...KEEP A HOT-WATER THERMOS ON YOU...

...SO YOU'RE PREPARED TO SPLASH HIM AT ANY TIME.

WE HAVE NO CHOICE BUT TO USE THESE.

WHEN YOU WASH YOUR HANDS, DRINK WATER, GO OUT IN THE RAIN...

THE SLIGHTEST BIT OF COLD WATER WILL CAUSE YOU TO TRANSFORM.

YOU TAKE PLENTY OF CARE TOO, JIJI.

YOU GOT THAT RIGHT.

I DON'T EVER WANT TO DEAL WITH IT AGAIN.

WE'VE GOTTA BE VIGILANT...

...UNTIL WE CAN COMPLETE THE EXORCISM!

WHERE WILL YOU LIVE, SHRIMP ALIEN?

I'LL BE LIVING AND WORKING AT A NEARBY DAIRY FARM.

THANKS TO MISS SEIKO.

IS IT AN ANTI-GRAVITY PROPUL-SION SYSTEM?!

HOW DOES THAT UFO ACTUALLY FLY?!

IT'S 🍤🍴🛸!

IF ANYTHING COMES UP, FEEL FREE TO CALL ON ME AGAIN.

THANKS FOR COMING TO OUR RESCUE!

HOOH! HOOH!

BY THE WAY, SHRIMP, SIR...

WHAT'S YOUR NAME?

ER...

ON EARTH IT WOULD BE PRO-NOUNCED...

UM, MR. SHRIMP?!

...PEENY-WEENY.

LOVE

SURE!

PLEASE LET ME RIDE IN YOUR UFO SOME TIME, MR. SHRIMP!

WELL, SEE YOU LATER, MR. SHRIMP!

IS EVERY-BODY IN?

SEE YA LATER, L'IL CHIQUI!

GET LOST, SHRIMP!

HATE

ODEN LOVE

NORMALLY I'M FINE JUST BEING COMPLETELY NAKED!

AW, SHUT UP!

TARO, YOU PUT THIS SHIRT ON INSIDE OUT!

I GOT THEM TRANSFERRED HERE TO KAMIKOSHI CITY.

HOW FAR IS IT TO THE HOSPITAL WHERE JIJI'S PARENTS ARE?

IT'S ABOUT TEN MINUTES AWAY.

BUT WHY IS HE STANDING LIKE A BOARD?!

TARO, YOU NEED TO GET THAT BODY MOVING PROPERLY!

THANK GOODNESS!

THEY SEEM WELL!

YUP!

THAT'S EASY FOR YOU TO SAY, BUT MOVING THE BODY BY ITSELF AIN'T EASY!

HOW OFF-PUTTING.

GAH! YOU'RE MAKING A MESS OF IT!

GIVE ME BACK MY BODY!

SYNCH UP THE MOVEMENTS WITH JIJI!

AT PRESENT, THE WILDFIRES ARE ALSO UNDER CONTROL...

HOWEVER, THE LEVEL FOUR ALERT WILL CONTINUE TO REMAIN IN EFFECT.

THERE WERE NO CASUALTIES FROM THE ERUPTION.

...HAVE BEEN ARRESTED ON SUSPICION OF MURDER AND ABDUCTION.

IN RELATED NEWS...

JUICHI KITO AND TEN OTHERS LIVING IN DAIJA, AKA SERPENT CITY...

n/Murder suspects arreste

POLICE ARE SEEKING HER WHERE-ABOUTS.

...IS CUR-RENTLY ON THE RUN.

NAKI KITO
SUSPECTED
RINGLEADER

FURTHER-MORE, THE SUSPECTED RINGLEADER, NAKI KITO, AGE UNKNOWN...

HEF!

HEF!

HEF!

MOMO AYASE!

YOU WON'T GET AWAY WITH THIS!

SHIT!

AND AFTER SPENDING 200 YEARS GETTING IT THAT BIG!

LET'S WALK TOGETH-ER!

OKARUN!

MISS AYASE! GOOD MORNING!

AWW, NOT GREAT!

HOW WERE THINGS WITH JIJI AFTER?

THE EVIL EYE SEEMS TO BE GETTING USED TO THE BARRIER.

DUNNO.

SOUNDS LIKE IT'S NOT AN ORDINARY EXORCISM.

WHEN DO YOU THINK THE EXORCISM WILL HAPPEN?

51. We Can All Stay There Together!

YOU KNOW THOSE HAYASHI PERFORMERS THEY HAVE AT, LIKE, FESTIVALS AND STUFF?

THEY'RE NEEDED IN ORDER TO KEEP THE EVIL EYE ENTERTAINED.

APPARENTLY THAT MAKES IT EASIER TO EXPEL IT FROM THE BODY.

WE'LL HAVE TO KEEP IT IN CHECK OURSELVES.

SO IF TARO'S BARRIER STOPS BEING EFFECTIVE, THEN WE'LL HAVE TO DEAL WITH THE EVIL EYE AGAIN?!

BUT IT SEEMS LIKE THERE AREN'T ANY AROUND TO PERFORM THE HAYASHI MUSIC FOR US.

BY THE WAY, THERE'S A FAVOR I WANTED TO ASK, OKARUN.

WHAT'S THAT? AN ALIEN?

HUH? WHAT ABOUT THE GIANT EARTHWORM?

V!! News

Volcanic Eruption! Is That A UFO?

LOOK, SEE!

THEY'RE SAYING A UFO WAS NEAR IT!

...SHE WON'T GIVE ME ANY MONEY FOR A PHONE.

MY GRANDMA BUYS MY UNIFORMS AND STUFF, BUT...

DON'T GOT ANY DOUGH!

I COULDN'T GET A HOLD OF YOU!

ANYWAY, WOULD YOU BUY A NEW CELL ALREADY?!

PLEASE DON'T BADMOUTH MOMO AYASE.

I WAS THE ONE WHO SPREAD THOSE LIES.

!!!

AIRA, WHAT'S UP?

GOT A SEC TO CHAT?

COME WITH US.

CUT THE ACT.

W-WHAT IS IT...

...MISS AYASE?!

LET'S GO. QUIT GRIPING ALREADY!

SHUT IT!

LET GO OF ME!

WHAT'RE YOU GONNA DO?!

I MEAN, JUST THE THOUGHT OF IT...

THIS IS THE WORST!

... MAKES ME SICK.

CAN'T BE HELPED.

WELL, I GUESS THERE'S NO OTHER WAY...

THIS TOTALLY SUCKS!

WHY HAS IT COME TO THIS?!

AGH! NO, NO, NO!

...

C'EST LA VIE, AS THEY SAY...

I GUESS IT'S UNAVOIDABLE, HUH?

WE'LL DO IT!

IF YOU CAN'T, THAT'S FINE. I'LL—

AIRA, IF YOU'VE GOT PLANS WITH FRIENDS, YOU CAN COME OVER WHENEVER.

HOW ABOUT STARTING TONIGHT?

TONIGHT?!

COOL!

HUH?! WHAT DO I DO?!

...YOU DON'T HAVE TO FORCE YOURSELF TO HANG OUT WITH ME.

AIRA. IF SOMETHING'S GOING ON BETWEEN YOU AND YOUR FRIENDS BECAUSE OF ME...

HUH?

NO...

I DON'T NEED TO HEAR THAT FROM YOU.

NOTHING LIKE THAT.

...

IT'S MY FAULT...

YOU'VE GOT NOTHING TO DO WITH IT.

AH!

THE ARM'S COME OFF.

JIJI, FROM HERE ON OUT, YOU'LL HAVE NO SUPPORT.

YOU NEED TO BE EVEN MORE CAREFUL OF WATER THAN YOU HAVE BEEN.

ONLY WASH YOUR HANDS IN HOT WATER.

RIGHT!

YOU SAVED ME!

THANK YOU, TARO!

GEEZ, AM I BUSHED!

I'VE BROUGHT THE WHOLE GANG.

PARDON THE INTRUSION!

I'M HOME!

AH.

YOU'RE BACK. PERFECT.

PRICEY!

COULD YOU LET ME USE SOME LATER?

SKK GOLD EXPERI-ENCE.

WHAT SKIN LOTION DO YOU USUALLY USE?

SURE THING.

IN THAT CASE, LET'S ALL PLAY TOGETHER.

I'M REAL GOOD.

OKARUN, LET'S PLAY SMASH BROS. AFTER.

MASSIVE BATTLE!

I TOLD YOU, I DON'T KNOW WHERE IT IS!

MY FLUFFY CUSHION.

MOMO.

AH. YES.

HEY, FOUR-EYES, PASS THE SOY SAUCE.

I AM SOOO SORRY.

COME ON. DON'T SAY THAT.

THIS IS HARD FOR JIJI TOO.

...TO USE HOT WATER WHEN WASHING YOUR HANDS!

AND AFTER TELLING YOU OVER AND OVER...

HOW MANY TIMES UNTIL YOU'RE SATIS- FIED?!

WHY, YOUUU!

SMACK

SMACK

THIS IS THE HOME OF SEIKO AYASE, ISN'T IT?

WELL, WE'RE HERE TO FULFILL YOUR REQUEST.

OH, I SEE!

SO WHAT IF IT IS?

WE'RE THE HAYASHI PERFORMERS.

IS THIS A JOKE?

THEY'RE SO COOOL!

WICKED! THEY'RE NOT WHAT I EXPECTED ...

I'M KINDA EXCITED!

BUT THEIR PERFORMANCE IS THE REAL DEAL.

THEY HAVE THE POWER TO MAKE THEIR SOUND REACH EVEN THE REALM OF THE DEAD.

SO THEY'RE SPIRIT MEDIUMS?

NO.

THEY'RE NOT EVEN SPIRIT SENSITIVE.

HUH?

PLUS, THE LESS SPIRIT SENSITIVE THEY ARE...

...THE LESS LIKELY THEY ARE TO BE WON OVER BY EVIL SPIRITS DURING THE EXORCISM.

53. We Became a Family

STOP IT!!

MOMO! HOLD JIJI STILL!

KEEP YOUR DISTANCE AND USE YOUR POWERS!

!!!

UNDER-STOOD!

HE JUST WANTS SOMEONE TO PLAY WITH!

HE JUST...

...ALL HE'S DREAMED OF IS THAT ONE DAY SOMEONE WOULD PLAY WITH HIM...

HE'S PRAC-TICED DANCING...

HE'S BEEN LOCKED AWAY FOR AGES...

...BUT EVEN STILL...

...IT'S ONLY TO GET KILLED AGAIN?!

...AND NOW, JUST WHEN HE THINKS HE'S FINALLY FREE...

I'LL BE SUPER CAREFUL NOT TO TOUCH ANY COLD WATER!

I'LL DO MY ABSOLUTE BEST!

DON'T KILL HIM! DON'T KILL THE EVIL EYE!

SO, PLEASE...

I'M *BEGGING* YOU!

I'M *BEGGING* YOU!

HUH?!

I'VE CHANGED MY MIND.

THE EXORCISM'S OFF.

THERE'S JUST SOMETHING I LIKE...

...ABOUT WHEN JIJI SHOWS SPIRIT LIKE THAT.

IT'S THE WAY IT'S GOTTA BE.

YOU HEARD WHAT JIJI SAID.

GRANNY, ARE YOU SURE?!

WELL, YOU CAN COUNT ME OUT!

SO, WHAT? WE'VE GOTTA KEEP WATCH OVER HIM FOREVER NOW?

I DON'T WANT TO WASTE IT ON HIS SELFISHNESS!

OUR TIME IS PRECIOUS.

IN THAT CASE...

...I'LL IMPROVE MYSELF ENOUGH THAT I CAN KEEP THE EVIL EYE IN CHECK.

IF I CAN GET TOUGH ENOUGH...

...IT WON'T BE A PROBLEM.

...THEN EVEN IF YOU DO MORPH...

YOU'D NEVER BE ABLE TO SLEEP PEACEFULLY AGAIN!

YOUR LIFE WOULD BE IN DANGER!

BUT THAT'S...

TAKAKURA, YOU'D GO TO ALL THAT EFFORT FOR HIM?!

SIT LIKE YOU'VE GOT ROOTS GROWING DOWN INTO THE GROUND.

TRY NOT TO FALL OVER EVEN WHEN PUSHED.

THUD

Y-YES, MA'AM!

AGH!

HARD EVEN. I DON'T MIND.

HUH? REALLY?!

JIJI, LIKE THIS.

BACK LIKE A ROD.

...

HERE GOES.

TRY TO PUSH ME.

PRETTY GOOD, CONSIDERING YOU USED TO GRUMBLE ABOUT PRACTICING IT BACK IN THE DAY.

WHOA! YOU'RE NOT FALLING!

WELL, I NEVER THOUGHT IT WOULD BE OF ANY USE.

SERIOUSLY?! THAT'S SO COOL!

IT'S HOW I CAN USE SUPERPOWERS.

YUP.

WAIT, IS THIS RELATED TO THAT WEIRD POSE YOU DID BACK IN ELEMENTARY SCHOOL?!

IF YOU CAN REACH THIS STATE, YOU'LL BE ABLE TO ACCESS YOUR SPIRITUAL POWER.

IT'S IN THIS STATE THAT ONE'S CHI EMERGES.

THE CARD-
BOARD'S
COME OFF
HERE.

HEY.

SURE.

THANKS,
OKARUN.

THERE'S
EVENING
DEW.

STAY
AWAY
FROM IT,
JIJI.

...I
CAUSED
A LOT OF
TROUBLE
FOR MISS
AYASE
AND THE
OTHERS.

WHEN
I WAS
CURSED
BY TURBO
GRANNY...

THIS IS ALL
MY FAULT.
I'M SORRY.

BUT THEY
WENT OUT
OF THEIR
WAY TO
SEE I WAS
TAKEN
CARE OF.

PLEASE
DON'T
APOLO-
GIZE.

WE'RE
ALL IN THIS
TOGETHER.

WHAT'S THE POINT OF PAYING ME BACK? MORON.

I PROMISED MYSELF I'D PAY BACK...

...THE LIVING EXPENSES AND CLOTHING COSTS, ET CETERA...

BUT THEN...

...SO I DELIVERED NEWSPAPERS AND BROUGHT HER SOME MONEY.

...YOU CAN PAY IT FORWARD BY HELPING SOMEONE ELSE WHO'S IN TROUBLE.

...FOR LOOKING AFTER YOU...

IF YOU'RE FEELING INDEBTED TO ME...

THAT'S WHAT BEING IN THIS TOGETHER REALLY MEANS.

BUT I'D LIKE TO BECOME EVEN A *LITTLE BIT* COOLER...

...SO I COULD BE LIKE HER.

I WISH I COULD SAY STUFF LIKE THAT...

DAMN, SHE'S SO AWESOME!

...BUT IN MY CASE, I'D JUST BE TRYING TO LOOK COOL.

CHIRP CHIRP CHIRP

YAWN!

ONLY CUZ I HATE INJUSTICE.

YOU, LIKE, FIGHT WITH YOUR SUPERIORS AND STUFF.

MOMO, YOU DON'T LAST LONG AT PART-TIME JOBS.

DIDN'T RIRINA SAY HER WORK WAS LOOKING FOR PART-TIME HELP?

SHE DID. A RES-TAURANT, RIGHT?

SO COOL!

FOR REAL?! PLEASE TELL HER I'LL WORK SUPER HARD!

I WON'T SWEAT THE SMALL STUFF!

I'M GROWN-UP NOW!

IT'LL BE OKAY!

IT'S HARD FOR SOMEONE TO RECOMMEND YOU FOR A JOB IF THEY THINK YOU'RE JUST GONNA QUIT RIGHT AWAY.

BING BONG

I HEARD THAT, MISS MII.

DID YOU HEAR THAT, MISS KEI?

NO, IT WOULD NOT.

SO IF MOMO AND JIJI HAD TEA TOGETHER, WOULD *THAT* BE A DATE?

WOULDN'T YOU CALL THAT A DATE?!

WE'RE JUST GOING TO HAVE SOME TEA!

I DON'T GO ON DATES!

THEN WHAT'S THE DIFF, YOU PIECE O'...?!

MRF MRF MRF!

FINE! DON'T HAVE A SINGLE DROP THEN!

I WON'T!

I WON'T DRINK A SINGLE DROP OF TEA!

YOU'LL GET THIRSTY.

OKARUN! RIGHT HERE, RIGHT HERE!

I WILL NOT!

OKA-RUN!

WHUT THE...

MISS AYASE!

AAH!

THREE!

HOW MANY IN YOUR PARTY?

WELCOME BACK, MASTER!

....!

HEY, MAID LADY!

SERVE THIS CUS- TOMER!

EXCUSE ME. THAT MAID'S GOT A BAD ATTITUDE.

FINE. WELC'M.

THIS WAY.

MISS AYASE! BE MORE COURTE-OUS!

AND SPEAK CLEARLY!

YES, MA'AM...

WELCOME TO OUR ESTAB-LISHMENT, YOU SACK OF SHIT.

SORRY! IT SLIPPED OUT!

YOU'RE SUPPOSED TO SAY, "WELCOME BACK"!

MISS AYASE! HOW COULD YOU?!

MOE!

MOE!

TRI-
BEAM!

YOU BASTARDS! YOU'LL REGRET THIS, DAMN YOU!

I TOOK SOME ADORABLE PHOTOS OF YOU, MOMO!

NICE WORK YOU'RE DOING THERE!

WHO CARES?! YOU'RE A MAID!

YOU'RE SO CUTE!

YOU TOLD ME THE JOB WAS AT A RESTAURANT!

DID YOU JUST COME HERE TO MAKE FUN OF ME?!

55. Moe! Moe! Tri-beam!

WHAT'S UP?

OKARUN, LET'S GO.

ACTUALLY, I'M GOING TO STAY...

GIVE IT YOUR ALL!

SEE YA. THANKS FOR YOUR SERVICE.

SHOO!

SHOO!

LEAVE! GO!

YOU'RE ON THE ROAD TO RENOVATING!

JIJI WILL BE WAITING FOR YOU.

OKARUN, YOU GOTTA GET OUTTA HERE ASAP.

HMMM?

HAVE FUN!

MISS AYASE, WHAT TIME ARE YOU HERE TILL?

GEEZ, IT'S COLD!

UH... TEN.

SORRY FOR BARGING INTO YOUR PLACE OF WORK.

YOU SHOULD BE!

DON'T EVER COME HERE AGAIN!

HUH?!

ALL RIGHT. THEN I'LL STAY HERE UNTIL YOU'RE DONE.

IT'S DANGEROUS FOR A GIRL TO GO HOME...

...ALONE AT NIGHT.

AND IT'S FREEZING. YOU'LL CATCH A COLD!

NO. I TOLD YOU TO LEAVE.

TAKE CARE.

OKAY, THEN...

I'LL BE FINE.

I'M TOUGH.

NUH-UH!

I... SEE...

REALLY ?!

MOMO, YOU WERE REALLY GREAT TODAY!

THANK YOU FOR EVERY- THING!

SEE YOU AGAIN SOON, OKAY?!

I'M SORRY FOR ALL THE HEADACHES I CAUSED YOU!

YUP!

I'LL BE OFF, THEN!

TAKE CARE!

HUH. GUESS I'LL HEAD HOME, THEN.

ALL DONE WITH WORK?!

HUFF HUFF

HUH?!, WAIT. YOU DIDN'T GO HOME?!

HUFF HUFF

MISS AYASE!

NOW LET'S GET HOME QUICKLY!

I CAN'T VERY WELL LEAVE A GIRL BY HERSELF AT THIS HOUR!

BRR, IT SURE IS COLD!

BECAUSE IT'S COLD.

IT'LL BE OKAY.

BELIEVE IN YOUR-SELF.

OKAY. HERE WE GO.

THAT TOTALLY DRAINED ALL MY STRENGTH!

YIKES!

AMAZING! IS SUCH A THING EVEN POSSIBLE?!

THAT WAS CLOSE!

YOU'RE A REAL PRODIGY, YOU KNOW.

UN-REAL.

...BUT COLD ONES ARE STILL OUT.

YOU MAY BE ABLE TO HANDLE ROOM TEMPERATURE LIQUIDS...

DON'T DROP YOUR GUARD.

IT SEEMS YOU'LL BE ABLE TO RETURN TO NORMAL LIFE.

AT LEAST IT'S GOOD TO KNOW YOU'RE CAPABLE OF SUPPRESSING IT.

EVIL EYE! STOP!

FIGHT ME INSTEAD!

BZAK

56. Feeling Kinda Gloomy

I'LL HAVE SOME OF THIS HOT WATER, IF I MAY.

THAT WAS CLOSE!

THANK GOD I DIDN'T SWALLOW IT!

I... CAN'T BELIEVE I DID THAT!

MOMO! I'M SO SORRY!

IT'S OKAY! IT'S OKAY!

IT WASN'T YOUR FAULT.

IT'S ALL RIGHT.

UH, IF I HELP, WILL YOU MAKE ME YOUR APPRENTICE?

THERE'S NO TIME TO BE PUTTING YOUR FEET UP.

EH?!

ANYWAY, COULD YOU TAKE THESE BAGS OVER THERE?

NO WAY.

WHY NOT ?!

WEEZ WEEZ

I WON'T... LOSE HEART!

NOT ME...

TOMORROW, I'LL GET HIM TO TEACH ME TO PUNCH FOR SURE...

I'M BACK!

BUT THAT MOVE WON'T WORK AGAIN.

WE MANAGED SOMEHOW THIS TIME THANKS TO MISS MOMO'S QUICK WITS.

I MEAN, TRYING TO LIVE WITH AN EVIL SPIRIT IS WEIRD IN THE FIRST PLACE.

AGREED?

I'LL GO CONTACT THEM.

MANJIRO.

LET'S CALL FOR THE HAYASHI BAND AGAIN.

IF YOU WON'T PERFORM THE RITUAL PRAYER, MASTER...

...THEN I WILL.

IT'S A BITTER PILL.

IT'S ALSO AN ADULT'S RESPONSIBILITY...

...TO SHOW THEM REALITY.

AS AN ADULT, YOU WISH YOU COULD SHOULDER ALL YOUR KIDS' BURDENS YOURSELF...

...AND TELL THEM...

LOOK, I ADMIRE JIJI'S SPIRIT TOO.

BUT WHAT CAN'T BE DONE CAN'T BE DONE.

...TO DO WHATEVER THEY WANT.

HOW SAD...

EMPLOY A SNAPPING MOTION AND...

WHAT DANCE IS *THAT*?

LISTEN, YOU. WHY'RE YOU TRYING TO LEARN TO PUNCH?

BECAUSE I WANT TO TOUGHEN UP, OBVIOUSLY!

CLUMSY SON OF A...

PFFT!

I'M NOT DANCING!

LEAVE ME ALONE!

IT'S THE SAME.

I WANT TO LEARN...

...TO THROW A PUNCH SO I CAN BECOME STRONG.

OR DO YOU WANNA BECOME STRONG?

SO DO YOU WANNA LEARN HOW TO THROW A PUNCH?

NO. THEY'RE DIFFERENT THINGS.

THE EVIL EYE IS LEVELS ABOVE YOU IN POWER AND TECHNIQUE.

JUST BECAUSE YOU CAN THROW A PUNCH DOESN'T MEAN YOU'LL BE STRONG.

WHAT ?!

SO THEN WHAT AM I SUPPOSED TO DO?!

HE CAN EVEN KEEP UP WITH MY POWER.

HIS SPEED'S CONSIDERABLE TOO.

57. Scary Dudes at School

PLEASE DON'T TELL ANYONE ABOUT THIS!

FOR- GET HER.

THEN TELL ME WHAT YOU'RE DOING!

YOU FOLLOWED US?!

MISS SHIRA- TORI?!

TAKAKURA! WHAT ARE YOU DOING?!

STAY OUT OF IT, TURD BURGLAR!

I'M NOT LEAVING UNTIL YOU TELL ME!

BEAT IT, BLOCK- HEAD!

MISS SHIRATORI, YOU CAN'T COME WITH US!

BRING IT, DUM- DUM!

I'LL MURDER- IZE YA!

NEXT TIME YOU UNDER- ESTIMATE ME, I'LL PUNCH YOU IN THAT HAIRBALL YOU CALL A FACE!

YOU LITTLE SHIT DUMP- LING!

Y-YOU'LL
BE OKAY!

WE'VE
GOT YOKAI
POWERS
TOO, SO...

TAKA-
KURA,
I'M
SCARED!

THAT IS YOUR COMBAT RHYTHM.

LOOK AT THAT DUMMY JUMP.

HEY!

WHAT'RE YOU TRYING TO DO HERE?!

AND THIS...

...IS THE EVIL EYE'S RHYTHM.

RHYTHM?

THIS IS THE EVIL EYE.

THIS IS YOU.

TRUDUDAH TRUDUDAH TRUDUDAH

PLINK PLINK PLINK

GET IT?

TAKING YOUR JUMPS BEFORE AS AN EXAMPLE.

PLINK

IN THE TIME IT TOOK YOU TO JUMP AND LAND ONE TIME...

...WOULD HAVE COMPLETED FOUR DIFFERENT ACTIONS.

...THE EVIL EYE...

TRUDUDUDUDAH

WHERE'S IT COMING FROM?!

THAT NOISE!

AN OR- CHES- TRA?!

HERE?! WHAT'S HERE?!

IT'S SO LOUD, I CAN'T HEAR Y—

THEY'RE HERE.

WHOOO'S MAKING THAT NOISE?!

I CAN HEEEAR SOME IMPURE SOUNNNDS.

THEIR MUSIC NOTES ARE BOMBS!

YOU GOTTA DODGE THOSE!

YOU DUMB BAS-TARD!

GUH!

TAKA-KURA-SAMA!

THEY'LL RENDER YOU UNABLE TO MOVE!

AND DEFINITELY DON'T GET CAUGHT BY THE REST SYMBOLS!

YOU'RE TELLING US TO DODGE...

58. Symphony No. 6

SHE'S DODGING ALL OF THEM!

WOW! AIRA-CHAN IS AWESOME!

TUNK

THIS IS NO TIME FOR ADMIRA-TION!

YOU NEED TO DODGE LIKE THAT TOO!

AND I'M GOOD-FOR-NOTHING!

MISS SHIRATORI! SHE'S INCREDIBLE!

KOFF! KOFF!

HFF! HFF!

I'M NO BETTER!

BUT NOT AT ALL...

BWUH!

I THOUGHT I'D BECOME A BIT STRONGER...

I'VE FOUGHT A BUNCH OF TOUGH ENEMIES...

OH!

...AND I GOT INTO THE RHYTHM OF IT!

IT REALLY MOVED ME...

THERE *IS* SOMETHING! SOME MUSIC I HEARD RECENTLY!

SHIT! NO OPENINGS TO COUNTER-ATTACK!

EVEN WHEN I TRY EXTENDING MY HAIR...

...THE NOTES ARE HITTING IT SO IT DOESN'T REACH THEM!

Dandadan Vol. 7 End

BONUS

PLEA

HEY, MOMO! WHERE'S THE MILK?!

HOW SHOULD I KNOW?!

End

KITO FAMILY

TYPE: HUMAN (?)
HABITAT: HOT SPRINGS DISTRICT
WEIGHT: 140-180 CM

A MULTIGENERATIONAL CLAN OF SELF-PROCLAIMED GUARDIANS OF A CERTAIN HOT SPRINGS AREA. OPERATING UNDER THE GUISE OF LANDLORDS, THEY BEHAVE OUTRAGEOUSLY AND WITHOUT CONSIDERATION. RESIDENTS AVOID THEM. THEY HAVE CONNECTIONS IN THE POLICE FORCE, SO ANY COMPLAINTS ABOUT THEIR CRIMINAL ENDEAVORS GET COVERED UP.

NAKI

JUMANUEL

JURIA

JUGEMU

JUHIKO

JUICHI

TYPE:
SUBTERRANEAN

HABITAT:
AGARTHA

HEIGHT:
180 CM (APPROX.)

SUBTERRANEAN

THE TRUE FORM
OF NAKI KITO, CURRENT HEAD OF THE KITO
FAMILY. ALL OTHER INFORMATION ABOUT HER
IS A MYSTERY.

YUKINOBU TATSU

I was overexuberant
in my chewing of some
Black Black gum, and
somehow my tolerance
for its spiciness has
now increased.

Yukinobu Tatsu debuted in
Gekkan Shounen Magazine with
Seigi no Rokugou (Rokugou of
Justice). He has also worked as an
assistant for manga artist Tatsuki
Fujimoto on the well-known series
Chainsaw Man and *Fire Punch*.

SHONEN JUMP Edition
Story & Art YUKINOBU TATSU

Translation/KUMAR SIVASUBRAMANIAN
English Adaptation/JENNIFER LEBLANC
Touch-Up Art & Lettering/KYLA AIKO
Design/JULIAN [JR] ROBINSON
Original English Logo Concept/SARA LINSLEY
Editor/JENNIFER LEBLANC

DANDADAN © 2021 by Yukinobu Tatsu
All rights reserved.
First published in Japan in 2021 by SHUEISHA Inc., Tokyo.
English translation rights arranged by SHUEISHA Inc.

The stories, characters, and incidents mentioned
in this publication are entirely fictional.

Printed in Canada

Published by VIZ Media, LLC
P.O. Box 77010
San Francisco, CA 94107

10 9 8 7 6 5 4 3 2 1
First printing, April 2024

viz.com

JoJo's

BIZARRE ADVENTURE

PART 5 *Golden Wind*

STORY & ART BY
HIROHIKO ARAKI

A MULTIGENERATIONAL TALE OF THE HEROIC JOESTAR FAMILY AND THEIR NEVER-ENDING BATTLE AGAINST EVIL!

GOLDEN WIND is here! The highly-acclaimed fifth arc of Hirohiko Araki's *JoJo's Bizarre Adventure* shifts the action from Japan to Italy, as Koichi Hirose heads to Europe to find an aspiring gangster named Giorno Giovanna, the secret son of Dio Brando, scourge of the Joestar family. Organized crime meets family drama and unbelievable enemy Stands in *JoJo's Bizarre Adventure: Part 5—Golden Wind*!

Hell's Paradise

JIGOKURAKU

**STORY AND ART BY
YUJI KAKU**

Gabimaru the Hollow is one of the most vicious ninja assassins ever to come out of the village of Iwagakure. He's ruthlessly efficient, but a betrayal results in him being handed a death sentence. There is only one hope: travel to a long-hidden island and recover an elixir that will make the shogun immortal and he will regain his freedom. Failure is not an option—on this island, Heaven and Hell are a hair's breadth away.

Even an invincible ninja may not be able to survive Hell's Paradise!

CAN MUSCLES CRUSH MAGIC?!

MASHLE

MAGIC AND MUSCLES

STORY AND ART BY
HAJIME KOMOTO

In the magic realm, magic is everything—everyone can use it, and one's skill determines their social status. Deep in the forest, oblivious to the ways of the world, lives Mash. Thanks to his daily training, he's become a fitness god. When Mash is discovered, he has no choice but to enroll in magic school where he must beat the competition without revealing his secret—he can't use magic!

Kafka wants to clean up kaiju, but not literally! Will a sudden metamorphosis stand in the way of his dream?

KAIJU NO. 8

STORY AND ART BY **NAOYA MATSUMOTO**

Kafka Hibino, a kaiju-corpse cleanup man, has always dreamed of joining the Japan Defense Force, a military organization tasked with the neutralization of kaiju. But when he gets another shot at achieving his childhood dream, he undergoes an unexpected transformation. How can he fight kaiju now that he's become one himself?!

RATED TEEN

VIZ

YOU ARE READING THE WRONG WAY

DAN DA DAN

Dandadan reads from right to left, starting in the upper-right corner. Japanese is read from right to left, meaning that action, sound effects, and word-balloon order are completely reversed from English order.